A Discovery Biography

Andrew Jackson

— ◆ —

Pioneer and President

by John Parlin
illustrated by William Hutchinson

CHELSEA JUNIORS
A division of Chelsea House Publishers
New York • Philadelphia

For Theresa and for her school children to read to her

The Discovery Biographies have been prepared under the educational supervison of Mary C. Austin, Ed.D., Reading Specialist and Professor of Education, Case Western Reserve University.

Cover illustration: Rick Daskam

First Chelsea House edition 1991

1 3 5 7 9 8 6 4 2

ISBN   0-7910-1442-8

Contents

Andrew Jackson: Pioneer and President

Chapter 1

Andy Reads the News

"The Philadelphia newspaper is here!" Andy Jackson shouted as he galloped up to a farmhouse. "I'm going to read it aloud at my uncle's house this afternoon."

Nine-year-old Andy rode his horse from farm to farm. He invited everyone in the little South Carolina settlement to hear him read the paper. Many of the grown people could not read. There had been few schools when they were children. But Andy was going to school.

Everybody wanted to hear the news. It was August, 1776. America had been fighting England for many months. England ruled America. But the Americans did not like the way the English ruled.

The Continental Congress was meeting in Philadelphia. The men in Congress were the leaders of America. What they did was big news.

The news had to travel a long way. A ship brought the newspaper from Philadelphia to Charleston. Then a postman on horseback rode 160 miles to the frontier where Andy lived. It was a place called the Waxhaw settlement.

Forty farmers came to hear Andy read the newspaper. Andy stood on a chair and read in a loud, clear voice.

He told how Congress had passed the Declaration of Independence on July 4th. The Declaration listed the things that England's King had done to America.

"*He has . . . burnt our towns and destroyed the lives of our people,*" Andy read.

"Down with the King!" one of the farmers shouted.

Andy held up his hand for silence. "I'm almost through," he said. "Just listen to this. *'These united colonies are and of right ought to be FREE AND INDEPENDENT STATES!'*"

"Hooray for freedom!" a farmer yelled. "And hooray for Andy! He's a good reader."

Andy stuck out his chest with pride.

There were some mighty big words in the Declaration of Independence. Andy had read each one right.

The farmers knew the Declaration of Independence meant a long war. Some of them had come to America from England. But they loved freedom more than they loved England.

Andy's father had come from Ireland. He had sailed to America before Andy was born. Andy's mother and brothers had come with him. The brothers were named Hugh and Bobby.

Mr. Jackson died in 1767. A few nights later, on March 15th, Andrew Jackson was born. His mother took the little baby and the older boys to live on the farm with their Uncle Jim and Aunt Jane.

Uncle Jim grew vegetables and raised cattle. When Andy was big enough he helped with the cattle. He built cow pens out of hickory wood. Andy used hickory because it was so hard and tough.

One morning soon after he read the newspaper, Andy decided to go fishing. His friend, George McWhorter, went with him. As they walked to the river they looked for Indian arrowheads.

Suddenly Andy spied one lying on the ground. George saw it at the same time. Andy dived for the arrowhead. But George got it first.

"That's mine!" Andy cried. "I saw it before you did!"

"No, you didn't!" George shouted. "I saw it first and I got it first. It's mine!"

Andy doubled up his fist and hit George on the jaw. He fought like a tiger. But George was bigger than Andy. He gave Andy a bloody nose.

The boys finally stopped fighting. But Andy still would not admit that George had seen the arrowhead first. Andrew Jackson always thought he was right.

When Andy got home his mother saw his bloody nose. She knew he had been in another fight.

"What makes you so hotheaded, son?" she asked.

"Maybe it's my red hair," Andy said.

"That's a poor excuse. Next time you get angry, count to ten before you start fighting. Maybe your temper will cool off."

"Suppose I were in the American army," Andy said. "Suppose I saw an English soldier coming down the road. Should I count to ten before I shot?"

"If you did, your aim would be better," his mother answered. "You'd have a better chance to hit him."

"But he might shoot me first," Andy said.

Andy was just daydreaming about the English soldier. The big battles were being fought in the North. However, the people in South Carolina helped by sending food to the army.

Chapter *2*

The War Comes Closer

When Andy was eleven, his Uncle Jim took him on a cattle drive to Charleston. Andy felt like a real man as he rode off from home. When a cow strayed from a herd, Andy galloped after it.

At night Andy sat by the campfire. The grownups often talked about Indian fights in the old days. A man told Andy that Indians sometimes made noises like birds to signal each other.

One night they heard an owl. It cried "whooo, whooo!" Andy's friend made the same sound. But it wasn't exactly the same. Andy learned to tell whether the "whooo" was made by an owl or a man.

Andy was excited when they reached Charleston. He had never seen such crowded streets, such big houses or so many buildings.

When Andy returned home, he heard that the war was coming closer. Some English soldiers had landed in Georgia. They were marching on Charleston.

The South Carolina soldiers were ordered to stop the English. Andy had an uncle who was a captain in the army. He was Uncle Bob. Andy's big brother, Hugh, was one of his soldiers.

Andy and his other brother, Bobby, begged Uncle Bob to let them join the army. But he said they were too young.

The American soldiers beat the English before they reached Charleston. But Hugh did not come back. He fought hard in the battle. Afterwards he became sick and died.

When Andy heard the news he cried. "Someday," he said to himself, "I'm going to make the English pay."

It wasn't long before the English came back. This time they captured Charleston.

Then some of them marched toward the Waxhaw settlement. They surprised some American soldiers near where Andy lived. They killed and wounded many Americans.

The Americans used the Waxhaw church for a hospital. The wounded men had to lie on the floor.

Mrs. Jackson, Andy and Bobby helped the wounded men. The boys brought water from a well. Then they built a fire and heated the water.

Their mother used the water to wash the soldiers' wounds. Some of the men cried with pain. This made Andy hate the English even more.

Later, he and Bobby went to see Uncle Bob again. "Please, Uncle Bob," Andy begged, "let us fight the English. We'll make good soldiers."

"How old are you, Andy?" Uncle Bob asked.

"I'm going on fourteen," Andy said. "And I'm big for my age."

"We need every man we can get," Uncle Bob said. "I'll be glad to have you."

Andy was proud that his uncle had used the word "man." Andy had played "soldier" when he was a little boy. Now he was a real soldier in a real war.

Chapter *3*

Prisoner of War

Uncle Bob heard that the English planned to attack the settlement again. He told his soldiers to meet at the church.

Andy and Bobby went by horseback to the church. As they waited for orders, they saw some farmers riding toward them. They thought the farmers were friends.

But they were not friends at all. The farmers suddenly stopped by the side of the road. Behind them many English soldiers were hiding. It was a smart trick. The English soldiers rushed toward the church. Their swords flashed in the sun.

The Americans fought bravely, but they were outnumbered. The English set the church on fire.

"Try to escape!" Uncle Bob shouted.

Andy and Bobby jumped on their horses. They raced off in different directions. An English soldier chased Andy. Andy and his horse jumped across a stream. Soon they were safe in the woods.

Suddenly, Andy heard a noise in the bushes. He held his gun ready to shoot.

It might be an English soldier. Before he shot, he remembered his mother's advice.

"One," he counted, "two, three . . ."

A horse's head poked out of the bushes. Sitting on the horse was Bobby. Andy was surely glad he had not shot!

That night, the boys camped in the woods. They had no food. The next morning they went to a cousin's house for breakfast.

While they were eating, some English soldiers broke into the house. They made the boys their prisoners.

One of the soldiers ordered Andy to clean his boots.

"Clean them yourself," Andy said. "I'm a prisoner of war! Not your slave!"

The English soldier lifted his sword.

Andy put up his hand to protect himself. The soldier hit Andy with all his might.

Blood poured from deep cuts on Andy's face and hand.

Later Bobby asked, "Wouldn't it have been better to clean his boots?"

"No!" Andy cried. "I'll never clean an Englishman's boots. They can hang me first!"

The English made the boys march 40 miles to a town called Camden. At Camden they were thrown into prison. Many other American soldiers were there.

Soon the boys caught a terrible disease. It was smallpox! Many prisoners died of smallpox.

Mrs. Jackson wanted to help her boys.

She came to see an English officer at Camden. She begged him to free Andy and Bobby. She said the Americans would free some English prisoners in return. The English let Andy and Bobby out of prison.

Mrs. Jackson took her sick boys home. Bobby died soon after they got there. Mrs. Jackson nursed Andy back to health.

There was more nursing for her to do. Some American soldiers were on English prison ships in Charleston harbor. The ships were dirty and crowded. Many soldiers were sick. Mrs. Jackson went to Charleston to nurse them.

When she kissed Andy good-by, she said, *"Never tell a lie, nor take what is not your own."*

It was the last advice she ever gave Andy.

One day, a horseman from Charleston brought Andy a small bundle. Andy opened it slowly. It held his mother's clothes and a few of her things.

His mother was dead. Andy was alone in the world.

Chapter *4*

By Wagon to Nashville

Andy was glad when the war was over. The Americans had won. Now Andy could make his living.

He decided to be a lawyer. He went to Salisbury, North Carolina, and studied in a lawyer's office.

After he learned to be a lawyer, he moved West. The Waxhaw settlement was getting crowded. A young man had a better chance to get ahead on the frontier.

Andy started for Nashville with some pioneers. They were the first group of people to take wagons over the new Cumberland Road. The road crossed 180 miles of forest. Wild Indians roamed the woods.

At night the pioneers camped by the road. One night some of the men sat up late singing around the campfire. Andy smiled as he listened.

"Way up yonder above the moon
A blue jay nests in a silver spoon.
Way down yonder on a hollow log
A red bird danced with a green
    bullfrog."

Just as the song ended Andy heard an owl cry "whooo." The cry came from north of the camp. Then Andy heard an answering "whooo" from the south.

Andy jumped to his feet. He knew the sounds were made by Indians, not owls!

He felt sure the Indians planned to attack when the men went to sleep. He rushed to the campfire and cried, "Indians are all around us!"

"What will we do?" one of the singers asked.

"We'll break camp now," Jackson said. "Wake everybody up."

The Indians were afraid to attack when everyone was awake, for all the men had guns. Andy was glad that he had learned how real owls sounded.

A few days later the pioneers reached Nashville. Andy looked at the small group of cabins.

"Where's the courthouse?" he asked someone.

"Over there." The man pointed to a tiny log building. It was only 18 feet square.

Soon Andy was busy working at the courthouse. He helped make the people obey the laws. Though he was only 21 years old, he was a good lawyer.

Andy moved into a boardinghouse run by Mrs. John Donelson. She had a beautiful daughter named Rachel. When she was only 17, Rachel had married a man named Lewis Robards. He was a bad husband. So Rachel came back to her mother's house to live.

Rachel thought Andrew Jackson was very handsome. He was six feet tall, and very slim. She and Andrew fell in love. They were married three years later.

Chapter *5*

The Big Horse Race

Jackson was very busy as a lawyer. With the money he saved, he bought a lot of land. He paid only ten cents an acre for some of it. He knew that some day his land would be worth a lot of money.

Many pioneers were moving to this part of the frontier. In those days it was called the "Territory South of the Ohio River." Jackson wanted it to become a state.

He and the other leaders made plans for the new state. They decided to call it Tennessee. Finally, the United States government approved their plan. Tennessee became the sixteenth state in the Union.

Now Tennessee must send men to be in the national government. Jackson was elected Congressman in 1796.

Rachel was proud that Andrew was going to Congress. But she was sad too. She would be lonesome without him.

"If only we had some children," she sighed as she kissed Andrew good-by. Jackson had to ride a horse most of the way to Philadelphia. That was where Congress met then. He was one of the first men in Congress to come from the frontier.

Some of the rich men from New York and Virginia made fun of Jackson's clothes. They laughed at the way he wore his hair. A long pigtail tied with an eel-skin hung down his back.

However, these men knew better than to laugh out loud. They had heard that Jackson had a hot temper.

When Jackson finished his work in Congress, he returned to Tennessee. He went back to being a lawyer. He also made a lot of money selling land.

Jackson was still interested in law. He became a judge. Many people said he was the best judge Tennessee had ever had. He also became a general in the Tennessee army. The Jacksons moved into a new house with a lot of land. They called it *The Hermitage*.

Jackson grew cotton and raised horses. His favorite horse was named Truxton. Truxton could run like lightning. But there was another fast horse in Tennessee. His name was Ploughboy.

Jackson and the man who owned Ploughboy decided to race their horses.

Jackson spent the days before the race training Truxton. One day a terrible thing happened. Truxton hurt his leg. Jackson's friends did not think Truxton had a chance to beat Ploughboy. They begged Jackson not to let Truxton race.

Jackson did not agree. He went up and patted Truxton's nose. "You'll be all right, boy, won't you?" Jackson said.

Truxton seemed to understand. Jackson decided to let him race.

The day of the contest was cloudy.

But hundreds of people came to the race track. The horse that won two out of three races would be the winner.

The first race began. Truxton got ahead of Ploughboy. His leg did not seem to bother him. The crowd cheered as Truxton won.

Then Truxton started limping. It did not seem possible that he could win the second race. Suddenly it started to rain. Perhaps the cool rain made the injured horse feel better. He went on to win the second race. That made it two out of three for Truxton.

Jackson was proud of him. And Rachel was proud of her husband. She knew that Jackson had given Truxton the will to win. In the future he would give many soldiers the will to win.

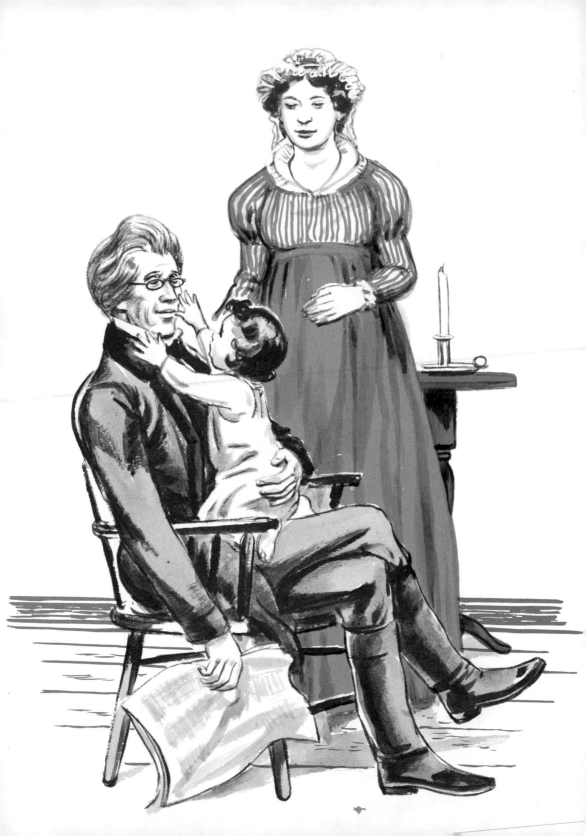

Chapter *6*

"Old Hickory"

Rachel and Andrew were happy at The Hermitage. They adopted a baby boy and named him Andrew Jackson, Jr.

Sometimes Jackson held the baby on his lap while he read the newspaper. The baby often tried to grab his father's glasses. This made it hard for Jackson to read.

The news in the papers was exciting. England and France were having a war. England needed every man she could get to help her fight.

English warships sometimes stopped American ships. The English took some of the American sailors to help them fight France. The English said the sailors on the American ships were really Englishmen.

The Americans were angry. America said England had no right to stop American ships at sea.

Jackson still hated the English. He was glad when America declared war on England. The war is called *The War of 1812* for that was the year fighting began.

Jackson ordered the Tennessee army to get ready to fight. They met near Nashville. It was terribly cold. There was not enough firewood to keep them warm.

One man said Jackson was not a good general because his men almost froze.

"You scoundrel!" Jackson cried. "More of that talk and I'll ram a red-hot poker down your throat."

Jackson and his soldiers were sent to the Mississippi River. They were to rush to New Orleans if it were attacked.

They camped by the river for a few weeks. Then they heard that the English were not ready to attack New Orleans.

Jackson and his soldiers started back to Nashville. The country was very wild. There were no roads and no bridges. Some of the soldiers were sick and could hardly walk.

General Jackson seemed stronger than any of his men. Sometimes he ran back and forth trying to cheer them up.

One day Jackson ran past a group of soldiers. One of the soldiers said, "Just look at the General. He surely is tough!"

"You're right about that," another soldier said. "He's about as tough as . . ."

"What?" a third soldier asked.

"Hickory! That's the toughest thing I can think of, especially if the hickory is old."

"Old Hickory," the first soldier said. "That's a good nickname for General Jackson."

From that day on Jackson was known as "Old Hickory" to his soldiers.

Chapter 7

War with the Indians

Jackson was not home long because soon there was trouble with the Indians.

The Indians were angry because the pioneers had taken some of their land. They wanted to get it back.

One tribe of Indians was led by a chief named Red Eagle. He thought the Americans were too busy fighting the English to fight the Indians too.

Red Eagle attacked Fort Mims, which was south of Tennessee. The Indians killed 250 Americans.

Jackson and his soldiers went after the Indians. There were several big battles which Jackson won. But each time, some Indians escaped to fight again. Red Eagle was always among them.

Red Eagle and his Indians had a town at Horseshoe Bend. It was protected on three sides by a river. The Indians built a wall out of logs on the fourth side. They cut holes in the wall to shoot through.

Jackson thought Red Eagle was at Horseshoe Bend. He was determined to catch him. So he and his men attacked the log wall. One soldier tried to climb it. The Indians killed him at once.

More soldiers rushed at the wall.

Some were killed, but others got to the top. They dropped down on the far side. They fought the Indians with guns and swords.

The Indians had guns too, as well as bows and arrows and tomahawks. They fought savagely. But slowly they were driven back toward the river. Many were killed.

Jackson sent a messenger to the Indians asking them to give up. The Indians shot at the messenger. So Jackson told his soldiers to fight harder.

Soon most of the Indians were killed or wounded. The few who were still alive hid in a small wooden fort. Jackson's soldiers used flaming arrows. They set the fort on fire. The Indians came out and the battle was over.

However, Red Eagle had not been killed. He had not even been at Horseshoe Bend the day of the battle. Jackson was disappointed.

A few days later a man came to Jackson's camp. He did not have a gun or a bow and arrow. He looked thin and hungry.

"Who are you?" Jackson asked.

"I am Red Eagle," the man said in a tired voice.

"You murderer!" Jackson cried. "You killed the women and children at Fort Mims."

"I have come to give myself up," Red Eagle said. "I am in your power."

"I ordered you brought to me in chains," Jackson said. "But you have come of your own free will."

"I have come to ask your help," Red Eagle said. "Not for myself. Not for my warriors. Most of them are dead."

"Then who do you want me to help?" Jackson asked.

"The Indian women and children," Red Eagle said. "They have been driven to the woods with nothing to eat. They are starving."

"I will send help to your women and children," Jackson promised. He and Red Eagle shook hands.

"Go!" Jackson said. "Find your warriors who are still alive. Tell them to live in peace."

Red Eagle walked out of the camp. He never made trouble again.

Chapter *8*

The Battle of New Orleans

Jackson had beaten the Indians. But war with England was still going on.

Late in 1814, Jackson heard that the English planned to attack New Orleans at last. New Orleans was an important port near the mouth of the Mississippi River. Jackson rushed his army to New Orleans. He was worried. He knew the English had many more soldiers than he had.

There were some pirates living on an island south of New Orleans. Their leader was named Jean Lafitte. The English were trying to get Lafitte to fight on their side. They promised him a lot of money.

Jean Lafitte said "No." He wanted to help the Americans.

"I am the Lost Sheep," he wrote, *"who desires to return to the flock."*

At first Jackson said he would not take help from pirates. But he needed all the help he could get.

One dark night, Jean Lafitte came to see him. "Perhaps we are outlaws," the pirate said, "but we are Americans too. My men know the land south of New Orleans. They can help you beat the English."

56

"All right," Jackson said. "We'll let you fight on our side."

A few days later the English landed south of the city. There were several small battles. Slowly the English came closer and closer to New Orleans.

There was a canal between the English and the city. It ran from the Mississippi River to a swamp. Jackson's soldiers made a wall on their side of the canal. The English would have to climb over the wall to capture New Orleans. Jackson and his soldiers hid behind the wall, and waited.

One night Jackson's spies had very important news. The English were going to attack early the next morning.

"Get ready to fight," Jackson told his soldiers.

The soldiers near the swamp were knee-deep in mud and water. They were wet and cold. Jackson came to cheer them up.

"How do you feel?" Jackson asked.

"Like we are half horses," one of the men said, "and half alligators."

Jackson laughed. He was glad his soldiers could joke before a battle. He felt sure they had the will to win.

Slowly, the sky grew light. But it was a foggy morning. The men could see only a little way.

Suddenly, the English sent up a rocket. Drops of fire fell in the fog.

Jackson knew it was a signal for the English to attack. He climbed on top of the wall and tried to see if the English were coming.

Just then a gust of wind blew the fog away. Jackson saw English soldiers marching toward the canal. Their white cross-belts stood out against their red coats.

"Pick your targets carefully," Jackson said, remembering his mother's advice. "Aim where the white belts cross. That way you'll hit the English soldiers' hearts."

"Fire!" shouted one of Jackson's officers.

"Crack! Crack!" went the guns.

"Boom!" thundered a cannon.

The English soldiers started falling. The field was dotted with their red coats.

A few of the Englishmen got across the canal. They leaped upon the wall.

It was no use. The Americans killed them or drove them back. The battle was soon over. The Americans had won.

Several weeks later, Jackson learned that the battle need not have been fought. A peace treaty had already been signed. But news traveled slowly in those days. Jackson and the English had no way of knowing that the war had ended.

However, the battle was important. It made the English respect the American Army. And it made Andrew Jackson a great American hero.

Chapter 9

Fighting in Florida

Three years after the Battle of New Orleans, Jackson went to war again. This time he fought the Seminole Indians in Florida. Florida belonged to Spain.

The Seminoles often crossed the United States border. They stole cattle and sometimes killed Americans. Spain should have punished the Indians. But she did not have enough soldiers.

Jackson marched his men into Florida. He heard that some Indians were at a Spanish fort at St. Marks. St. Marks is a town on the Gulf of Mexico.

When Jackson got to St. Marks, the Indians had fled. However, he did find an old Englishman named Arbuthnot.

"Have you helped the Indians?" Jackson asked.

"Yes," Arbuthnot admitted. "The English treat them badly. And you Americans rob them."

Jackson turned to one of his soldiers. "Arrest this man," he shouted. Arbuthnot was made a prisoner.

Then Jackson and his soldiers marched toward an Indian village on the Suwannee River. They hoped to capture the Seminoles there and teach them a lesson.

When they reached the Indian village, it was empty. The Indians had left.

Jackson and his soldiers made camp.

That night they captured an Englishman named Ambrister. He had a letter from Arbuthnot.

"The Americans are coming," the letter said. "Tell the Indians to hide."

Now Jackson knew why his long march had been useless. He arrested Ambrister and took him back to St. Marks. Jackson said that Ambrister and Arbuthnot were enemies of America. They should not have helped the Indians. He had the men tried. They were guilty.

Ambrister was shot and Arbuthnot was hanged. But Jackson did not see them put to death.

He had already started for Pensacola, the biggest town in West Florida. He and his soldiers had to march through the swamps and wade across the rivers.

Some of the soldiers were barefoot when they reached Pensacola. The Spanish were afraid of them. They soon gave up. The Americans took Pensacola.

When the King of Spain heard what Jackson had done, he was angry. He said the United States must give Pensacola and St. Marks back to Spain. He wanted Jackson punished. He said Jackson had no right to bring his army to Florida, or kill the Englishmen.

The two towns were given back to Spain. Then the United States offered five million dollars for all of Florida. Spain took it. Florida became United States territory. And Jackson was not punished. He was sent back to Florida. He was the first American Governor of the new territory.

Chapter *10*

Jackson Saves
the Union

Jackson was Governor of Florida for only a few months. Then he went to Washington as a Senator from Tennessee.

At first Rachel stayed at The Hermitage. Jackson missed her. But he became one of the most popular men in Washington. Many people said that Jackson should be President of the United States.

In 1824, he ran for President. He was defeated by John Quincy Adams. Adams was much better educated than Jackson. And his father, John Adams, had been President before him.

Jackson ran for President again in 1828. Children sang that the election was between:

"John Q. Adams who can write
And Andrew Jackson who can fight."

The people liked the man from the frontier who could fight. Jackson was elected.

He was the first President to come from one of the new states, west of the mountains. All the other Presidents had come from either Massachusetts or Virginia. They had been born into rich families.

Jackson was the first President to be born a poor boy. His election proved that every boy had a chance to be President.

Before Jackson moved into the White House, Rachel became sick. She died at The Hermitage just before Christmas.

Jackson was heartbroken. However, he was the new President. Rachel's niece and nephew, Emily and Jack Donelson, moved into the White House with him. They had a little boy named Andrew Jackson Donelson. Their baby girl was born in the White House.

One day a man came to see the President on important business. But the business had to wait. The baby was asleep in the President's arms. Jackson did not want to wake her up.

He always liked children. *"They are the only friends I have who do not pester me with advice,"* he once said.

And many grownups pestered him.

Men who had voted for Jackson flocked to Washington. They wanted jobs.

"To the victors belong the spoils," these men said. "Fire the people who worked under Adams. Give us their jobs."

Jackson did fire many people. But he tried to be fair.

Once a Congressman asked him to fire an old man who had fought with George Washington. Jackson's blue eyes flashed with anger. "That old man has a pound of English bullets in his body. He keeps his job."

Other men came to see Jackson about more important matters. Congress had passed a law that South Carolina did not like. South Carolina said that if she did not like a law, she would not obey it.

Many people tried to tell Jackson what to do about South Carolina. Some thought South Carolina was right. Others were sure she was wrong. At first, Jackson would not say what he thought.

One night he went to a big dinner party. He knew that what he said there would be in all the newspapers. He would tell the people what he thought.

At the end of the dinner, Jackson asked the men to stand up. They would drink a toast together.

The President lifted his glass. He said, *"Our Federal Union—it must be preserved!"*

He meant that South Carolina did not have a right to disobey laws made by Congress. If she did, the United States would break up. Jackson thought the government in Washington was more important than the state government.

Later he said that South Carolina had better not try fighting. If blood were shed, he promised to *"hang the first man I lay my hands on . . . upon the first tree that I can reach."*

Jackson meant what he said. South Carolina did not fight. The Union was saved.

Chapter *11*

A Strong President

One afternoon Jackson went to see Charles Carroll. It was Charles Carroll's ninety-fourth birthday.

Charles Carroll was the only man still alive who had signed the Declaration of Independence. The old man was pleased that the President had come to see him. "I am honored," he said.

"No," Jackson said. "I am the one who is honored. When I was a boy I read the Declaration aloud. I read it to the farmers in South Carolina."

Charles Carroll's old eyes sparkled.

"There were some mighty big words in the Declaration of Independence," Jackson said with a smile. "It was hard for a little boy to read."

Charles Carroll laughed. "That was Thomas Jefferson's fault," he said. "He wrote it."

"By signing it you helped make America free," Jackson said. "And all America thanks you."

Jackson had three big ideas about America. He believed that all the people should take part in the government. He believed that all the states should stick together. And he believed that the President should have a great deal of power. These beliefs helped Jackson get elected a second time. In his second term he certainly needed power.

He was against the United States Bank. This was not really a government bank. It was a private bank owned mostly by rich men. The United States kept its money in the bank. This helped the rich men get even richer.

"That is wrong," Jackson said. "The government's money should help all the people, not just the rich."

The men who ran the bank did not give in easily. One of them said, "Jackson may have killed Indians and Englishmen. But that does not mean he can kill our bank."

It was a hard fight. But Jackson finally won. The government's money went into state banks. This made it easier for ordinary people all over the country to borrow money.

Now Jackson's term in the White House was coming to an end. He did not run for President again. He helped his friend, Martin Van Buren, become the next President.

Jackson started on the long trip home. One night he stopped at a hotel. Some children came to his window and sang a song about him.

"If I were President of these
   United States,
I'd suck molasses candy and swing
   upon the gates.
Oh, glory be to Jackson
   For he played many pranks,
And glory be to Jackson
   For he blew up the banks."

Jackson came to the window and waved to the children.

He was happy when he reached The Hermitage. He ran the farm and wrote letters about government affairs.

In March, 1845, Jackson learned that Florida had become a state. This meant that the United States flag would have 27 stars.

"Just think," Jackson said to a friend. "The stars in our flag have more than doubled since our country was founded."

Jackson had helped add some of those stars. Now he was working to add Texas to the Union.

But Jackson was a sick man. He died on June 8, 1845.

All over America the flag flew at half-mast. The nation was in mourning for Old Hickory.